real-life stories

STREET CHILD

D0306803

Hamilton's Story

by Colin Hynson
Produced in association with
ChildHope UK and Estrela UK

WE WOULD LIKE TO THANK THE FOLLOWING FOR THEIR HELP IN THE PRODUCTION OF THIS BOOK:

Elanor Jackson from ChildHope, UK;
Julia McNaught from Estrela, Brazil; Nivaldo Ferreira da Silva from
Cultura em Movimento (Culture in Movement); Dona Aurenita Rodrigues;
Catherine Panter-Brick, University of Durham, UK; Jean Coppendale and Indexing Specialists (UK) Limited;

and our special thanks to

Hamilton

without whom this book would not have been possible.

Picture credits (t=top; b=bottom; c=centre; l=left; r=right): Corbis 27b, 29b, 35b, 31r;
Nivaldo Ferreira da Silva 25l, 37l; Exile Images 9t, 27t; Getty Images 41br; Impact Photos 25r, 33b; Julia McNaught 1, 3, 8, 10, 12, 13l, 15, 16, 18, 19l, 20, 22, 24, 26, 28, 30, 31l, 32, 34, 36, 38;
Magnum Photos 39t; Still Pictures 9b, 11b, 21t, 23b, 29t, 33t, 35t, 39b, 40l; Hamilton Correia Rodrigues 3;
World Image Library 4l, 5b, 6, 7, 9t, 11t, 13r, 15t, 15b, 19r, 21b, 23t, 37r, 40r, 41, 42, 43l, 43r, 44, 45.
Every effort has been made to trace the copyright holders, and we apologise in advance for any unintentional omissions.
We would be pleased to insert the appropriate acknowledgements in any subsequent edition of this publication.

THE INTERVIEWERS

The interview with Hamilton (the subject of the book) was conducted by Julia McNaught from Estrela and Nivaldo Ferreira da Silva from Cultura em Movimento (Culture in Movement) – both based in Salvador, Brazil. Estrela is a UK charity that works alongside and supports Brazilian youth and excluded groups. Cultura em Movimento is a prominent reggae/cultural organisation that stages many events in the Rocinha district.

The interview was co-ordinated by Elanor Jackson at ChildHope UK. ChildHope has implemented many schemes hat strive to prevent poverty, conflict and disease with a view to improving life for young people.

JULIA SAYS ...

"Doing the ground work for this book has revived many happy memories. It has also revived my conviction about the importance of ensuring that there are opportunities for young people who are so full of creativity, sensitivity, hope and a sense of freedom. Our world today needs people like them."

ELANOR SAYS ...

"Reading Hamilton's story a few years after ChildHope first knew him as a boy, provides a sense of hope for other street children. For in spite of all the hardships he has suffered, Hamilton displays such resilience, generosity and creativity – qualities that many more fortunate young people in the world lack."

Julia McNaught and Nivaldo Ferreira da Silva (known artistically as Aluminio) who conducted the interview with Hamilton.

CONTENTS

3

Introduction

Throughout the world, large numbers of children live on the streets. Many of these children do not go to school and do not have the love and support of a family in a warm, safe home. In order to survive, many must work, beg or steal. These children often have jobs where they could easily injure themselves, and they are particularly vulnerable to poor health, and attacks from other children and from adults. Every day these children face danger and some of them will lose their fight for survival. Large numbers die due to disease and poor health, and some are even murdered.

Children who live on the streets face many threats. Friends often stick together, opting for 'safety in numbers'.

WHO ARE THE STREET CHILDREN?

It is impossible to know for certain how many street children there are in Brazil at any one time. The main reason for this is that the millions of Brazilian children we loosely term 'street children' have quite different individual circumstances, causing them to fall into several different categories. For example, 'home-based children' is a term often used to define the children who spend a significant proportion of their time on the streets but who still have family homes that they can go to for support and as a place to eat and sleep. These children spend their days (or nights) working on the streets in order to help support themselves and their families.

'Homeless' children live and work on the streets generally because they have run away from their homes and do not feel they can return. They might have left their families to escape poverty or because a family member was hurting them.

Another group live and work on the streets because, for whatever reason, the ties between them and their parents have been cut off. These children can often be found in war-torn countries or where poverty is so great that parents find it impossible to care for their children.

WHY ARE THEY ON THE STREETS?

Children find themselves on the streets for all sorts of reasons. The main reason is simply that they come from a very poor background. They need to work in order to buy food and other essentials for themselves and their families. Other children are escaping from homes that are overcrowded. They might also be running away from domestic conflicts or because they have been forced to leave. Some children are separated from their parents in times of war, or become orphans and have nowhere else to turn.

COUNTRIES WITH HIGHEST NUMBER OF STREET CHILDREN WORLDWIDE

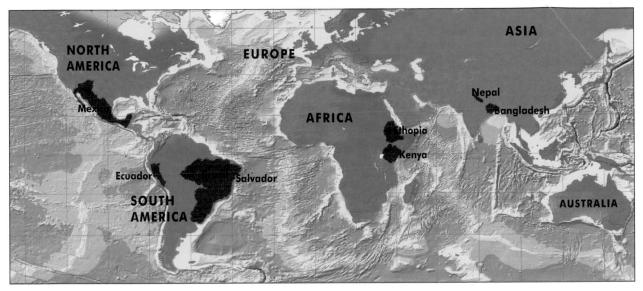

LIVING AND WORKING ON THE STREETS

There are many different kinds of jobs that children on the streets can take up. The more straightforward – though poorly paid – jobs include washing cars, running errands and shining shoes. Some of the jobs street children do can be dangerous. These include carrying drugs and prostitution.

Sleeping on the streets is a harsh reality for millions of children worldwide.

HOW MANY CHILDREN LIVE ON THE STREETS?

It is difficult to know the precise number of street children worldwide so it is important to recognise that the figures below are just 'guesstimates'. Some children work and play on the streets but still have homes to go to. Others have no homes to go to. Some children only live on the streets for a short time, while others keep themselves hidden, so it can be difficult to ever achieve an accurate figure.

Kenya:	250,000
Ethiopia	150,000
Nepal:	30,000
Bangladesh:	440,000
Mexico:	114,000
Ecuador:	10,000
Brazil:	7–8 million

Brazil is one of the most culturally diverse countries in the world. Brazilians descend from a wide variety of countries including Africa and Portugal.

THE PEOPLE OF BRAZIL

The original Brazilian settlers were Native American. Today, however, the majority of Brazilians are of Portuguese origin or are descended from African slaves. One third of all Brazilians are mixed-race, or "mulattoes" – usually a mixture of African and European. There are also a large number of Germans, Poles, Japanese, Italians and Germans. More recently people from Korea and the Middle East have moved to Brazil.

THE GROWTH OF BRAZIL'S CITIES

Brazil is rapidly becoming an urban society, as more people are born there or move in from the countryside. People from the countryside come to escape poverty, attracted by the promise of a well-paid job and a better life. Rural

BRAZIL – A BRIEF HISTORY

For centuries, Brazil was controlled by Portugal. Then, in 1822 Brazil became independent. For many years people in Brazil did not have many rights and free speech was not allowed. Through most of the late-20th century, Brazil was controlled by a military dictatorship. Then, in 1985, a civilian became president – this sparked the beginning of democracy in Brazil where human rights were gradually introduced. In 2002, Lula, the leader of the Workers' Party was elected president.

Brazil is a land of great contrasts. It is the fifth largest country in the world and has the tenth largest economy. The gap between rich and poor is one of the biggest in the world. The wealthiest 1 per cent of Brazil's population controls over 50 per cent of the country's wealth. The poorest 50 per cent receive only 10 per cent of the country's income.

BRAZIL – FACTS AND FIGURES

Population: 184 million.

Capital City: Brasilia.

Geography: Largest country in South America. Mostly forest and lowlands with some plains and mountains.

Climate: Mostly tropical but cooler in the south.

Religions: Brazil is 80% Roman Catholic which makes it the largest Roman Catholic country in the world. The rest are other Christian groups and African religions.

Literacy: One third of all Brazilians are illiterate.

Brazil has the tenth largest economy in the world.

migrants have large families which brings even more people into the cities. Today, about 80 per cent of Brazil's population live in urban areas. The United Nations estimates that by 2015, this will increase to nearly 90 per cent. The sheer volume of new people is putting a great strain on housing, jobs and transport. Many of these migrants remain poor and their children find themselves on the streets.

THE STREET CHILDREN OF BRAZIL

In a country with so much poverty, it is not surprising that there are so many children living and working on the city streets. However, many of the wealthier city-dwellers do not feel sorry for these children. Instead, they see them as a nuisance and a threat to their way of life.

Many businesses employ security guards to keep these children away from the areas where they work. Many police officers are similarly intolerant of street children – which has prompted the emergence of "death squads" – groups of police officers who illegally kill children just for being on the streets.

RECENT HISTORY TIMELINE

1964 Jõao Goulart, the elected president of Brazil is overthrown by the military. General Humberto Branco becomes the new leader of Brazil.

1968 Workers and students stage large demonstrations and strikes against the military government. The Church sides with the protesters. The military respond by suspending civil liberties. Opposition leaders leave the country.

1969–1974 Brazil enjoys an economic boom. However, all press is heavily censored and political opponents are tortured and imprisoned.

1979 The Workers' Party is formed to oppose the military government.

1985 Democracy is restored to Brazil.

1988 Fransisco 'Chico' Mendes, an internationally known environmentalist, is assassinated.

1989 The first free and fair Presidential election. It is won by Fernando Collor de Mello.

1992 President Collor charged with corruption.

1993 Fernando Henrique Cardoso elected president

2002 Lula, the leader of the Worker's Party, wins the presidential election

2003 Land reform begins with land being given to 400,000 poor families.

CHAPTER ONE: Meet Hamilton

Almost one quarter of Brazil's population live under the poverty line, earning less than US$80 per month. Desperation for money and food often drives the children of these families onto the streets to beg or find some kind of employment. For young people, the streets can be a way of escaping the hardships of their home lives. Hamilton Rodrigues is a young person who has spent a great proportion of his life so far on and off the streets.

HAMILTON SAYS ...

"My name is Hamilton Correia Rodrigues and I am 18 years old. I was born in Pelourinho, in Salvador, Bahia, Brazil. I am nothing – since I began life, right up until today. But I am a person, a human being. I'm cool, humble, fun and cheerful – that is what I am. I'm tall with black hair, now with designer details.

Other people see me as someone who does nothing in life. Adventuring into the day, selling something or other.

I can speak Portuguese, and a little bit of Spanish, Italian and English. I like studying, reading and capoeira (see page 15). My friends and I sometimes go to the beach for fun.

ALUMINIO SAYS ...

"Hamilton is someone who had a very low life expectancy – but he's a survivor of the streets. He's back at home now, still working the streets, selling souvenirs and having a good time.
I don't see him as a bad kid – rebellious, but not offensive. His fight for survival corresponds to the way he has been brought up."

Hamilton is a thoughtful, intelligent young man with a lot of passion and enthusiasm for life.

DONA AURENITA (HAMILTON'S MOTHER) SAYS ...

"Hamilton's my son. He used to run away from home, even in his underpants sometimes! He'd go after the vans with megaphones and loud music that would play those carnival songs. Loads of kids would go after them. He gave me a lot of trouble, it was terribly hard to try and get him to come back. Sometimes I'd go after him with clothes – a t-shirt and shorts. When he started going on the streets, I'd go to the Youth Justice, and once they told me he was in the juvenile lock-up, out at Tancredo Neves. I had many sleepless nights staying up and going after him."

MANY DIFFERENT REASONS

It is estimated that about 20 million children spend a great proportion of their time on the streets of the cities of Brazil. This figure includes a great number of children who are on the streets during the day and then return to their families at night. These children are usually working to bring some extra money to their poverty-stricken parents.

Besides those children who have a home to go to at night, there is also an estimated 7 to 8 million children for whom the streets are their home – both day and night.

For many children on the streets, the streets are their playground. These children often have homes to go to at night.

Most children on the streets feel they have no-one to turn to for help or support.

THE DAILY STRUGGLE

Street children face a daily struggle for survival. Not only do they have to find money for food and other necessities for survival, but they also face many dangers on the streets.

While a large number of children succumb to the many traumas, threats and afflictions that threaten their well-being, others survive and even carry on to create a better life for themselves. Living and/or working on the streets often instills an amazing resilience in these young people – many survive due to a strong character and determination to stay alive at all costs.

"I can read and write a bit – enough to survive. I used to go to school, the Mestre Pastinha School, for about four years. I liked the kids, the teachers, the snacks and playing around in the classroom. I also liked drawing. I didn't like tests though. I played truant loads – missed school to go and hang out and smoke on the streets. My favourite subjects were art and drawing. I'm actually thinking of going back to study more soon.

There was one really pretty teacher when I was at school – she was gorgeous. I saw her not so long ago, and she remembered me. My favourite book is by Jorge Amado. It's called, Gabriela, Clove and Cinnamon. Amado writes all about Bahia, our history and culture.

My best friends are my mum, my dad and my sister. I have a pretty good relationship with my family. My sister Bete and I are closest. We live together, we help each other. We fight but we're close. My oldest sister Naná lives in another neighbourhood with her husband and two children. We get on OK, but we're more distant.

On the streets my best friends were Jau (Jailton), Juquinha (Ricardo) and Itamar."

Hamilton aged 12 (at the back), with his friends Isaias, Gabriela and Moabe from Project Ibveji . The friends were performing at a street-theatre cultural event, organised by Project Altivaçao.

EDUCATION IN BRAZIL

It is compulsory for Brazilian children between the ages of seven and 14 to go to school although the law doesn't work in practice which is a major problem for Brazil. The children of poor families are much less likely to finish their education than children of wealthy families.

For children living on the streets, going to school is even more difficult, as they need to work during the day. Also, there are no adults on the streets to ensure children go to school or that they have the right clothes and equipment. Currently, four million children in Brazil do not go to school. Only 40 per cent of children who begin their primary education actually complete it. It is evident that education in Brazil is undergoing a crisis. There is a vast discrepancy in the standards of teaching and facilities between private schools in wealthier districts and state schools in poverty-stricken areas.

The luxury of school lessons with an abundance of resources (pictured) is a far cry from the over-crowded under-resourced classes available to slum children.

Tourism is a major source of industry in Brazil's cities. Many street children make a living selling to travellers.

THE TOURIST INDUSTRY

Brazil is becoming more and more popular as a tourist destination. The number of people who come to Brazil on holiday has risen from just over one million in 1990 to about four million in 2000. Nearly half of these visitors come from other South American countries, particularly neighbouring Argentina. Tourism provides over six million jobs, so it is a very important part of Brazil's economy. Many street children also rely on a regular influx of tourists to provide them with business.

Many holiday-makers come to Brazil to relax on the beaches or watch the carnivals. However, eco-tourism, when visitors come to see the Amazon jungle or the spectacular Iguacu Falls, is also becoming popular.

"My family are Afro-Brazilian. I am passionate about many aspects of my culture – such as, capoeira, samba, drumming and percussion – all things that have a connection to Africa. Bahia is the second Africa. We have the largest black population outside Africa.

I know a bit about the history of our people. I know we're the descendants of slaves. My mother is from Jacobina, inland Bahia. I have always lived in Bahia – today I live in the Rocinha, one of Pelourinho's surviving ghettos.

The festivals we celebrate include Carnival, St John's Festival, New Year and Christmas. At Carnival there is lots of adrenalin! Lots of women, poppers and music. I like going after the big trio elétricos (giant sound systems and bands on moving wagons) – and having a good time.

I like to do all sorts of things with my friends We used to play about on the streets or we'd go to the beach. The biggest adventure we ever had was when the police came after us and caught us – they'd seen us rob an old woman. They got hold of me and Jau by our shirts and were taking us off. I managed to wriggle my way out of my shirt, and the policeman ended up with my shirt in his hands! It was in Graça. When he realised he let go of Jau, and he got away as well!

I knew a lot of lads who were involved in burglaries and wanted us to get involved, too. I would just get up and go away when they started talking about it.

I believe in God – God in the heart – and I pray every night. I don't go to church regularly anymore. I used to go to the Baptist Church with my mother when I was little. However, it's no longer there.

For me, Jesus is the salvation, of all problems. God is salvation. I believe that when a person dies they see the book of their life. They then have to pay for what they did in their life on Earth – the good and the bad. Each person will then get what they deserve.

I am a person who likes to look for the good side in everything. I try and do good things, and I try to be peaceful and calm as much as possible.

I often imagine what it would be like to have a house of my own. The house of my life. In my own home, I would be able to live with my wife

Despite all the hardships he has endured, Hamilton remains passionate about his family and his culture.

Hamilton, aged 12 (third from left), and other members of Ibveji´s theatre group, preparing to join a march against racial violence and death squads.

and raise my child – like anybody – a worker. And my mother would live there too, if she's alive – God willing. Living with my mum makes me happy. Funny people also make me happy. People who are natural jokers or clowns – they really make me laugh. I like their attitude.

The happiest day of my life was when I was in Morro de São Paulo (tropical island beach resort) with four Spaniards, a caipirinha cocktail in my hand, and R$1,500 in my pocket!

I adore music … 'streetkids selling ice lollies, streetkids cleaning windscreens' [lyrics from a carnival song].I was part of Buscapé (a children's carnival group). I used to play with Mestre Prego and the Banda Meninos do Pelô – samba percussion – I would play the big drums."

FACTS – FESTIVALS AND CARNIVAL

Brazilians celebrate a wide variety of religious and non-religious festivals every year. Thousands flock to the streets to witness and join in with music, dancing, costumes and public religious ceremonies.

• Every June in Brazil, Roman Catholics remember the saints Anthony, Peter and John with huge outdoor firework parties known as *Festas Juninas*.

• Many festivals are celebrated by those who still practise the African faith known as 'Candomblé'. These highly ritualised events involve animal sacrifices, ritual clothing, dance and song.

• In Salvador, the 'Lavagem do Bonfim' festival has been celebrated every January since 1754. During this festival, a group of women dress all in white and carry long white vases on their heads filled with perfumed water and white flowers.

• Of the many non-religious carnivals that happen in Brazil during February and March, the most famous is Carnival which takes place in many cities, but the biggest parties take place in Salvador and Rio de Janeiro. The costumes, parades, music and partying all contribute to making Brazil the Carnival capital of the world.

Carnival is possibly the most important event in the Brazilian calendar – people party on the streets for days.

13

Street Child – *Hamilton's story*

"Loads of people lived on the streets like I did. I have four friends who lived on the streets with me, but there are many more. The good things about living on the streets were the friends and freedom. I liked playing about and being cheeky with the others. Most of all, the excitement is what appeals. The cold and the rain is probably the hardest thing.

We never really lived in one place on the street – but rather, we moved around a bit. I hung about in Campo Grande, Canela, Graça, Barra and Piedade – all central and wealthier districts of Salvador because otherwise my mother would catch me. I hung around with my friends Jau, Juquinha and Itamar. We used to sleep on top of bus shelters, behind kiosks, on the beach or in the park. It would depend which neighbourhood we were in. We used to eat leftovers – of hamburgers, chips, juice, pop. We used to go down to Lapa central bus station and get hot dogs. We'd beg them from people or ask for a bite, and if they didn't give us them, we'd just snatch them and run!

I feel angry when I speak and the person ignores me and doesn't pay any attention. There was no shortage of that when I was a kid. I hate people talking badly about one another. When I am sad or angry, I talk to my sister, Bete. I am generally a calm and happy person.

I like playing capoeira, and swimming, in the sea. And playing a bit of football sometimes, but I'm best at capoeira."

Hamilton's favourite pastime is capoeira – a kind of martial art that requires grace, agility and mental stamina.

RECREATION IN BRAZIL

The people of Brazil are very keen on sports – and they are particularly passionate about football. Street children can often be seen playing football in the favelas (public squares) and on the beaches of Rio de Janeiro. Brazil's greatest football hero, Pelé, is regarded internationally as the greatest footballer of all time, inspiring many young Brazilians to follow in his footsteps for decades to come. People also play volleyball on Brazil's beaches – the second favourite sport of Brazil. Other popular sports are tennis, basketball and surfing.

Each city has its own public holidays which are usually an excuse for everybody in the city, young and old, to mingle and enjoy themselves. Brazilians really know how to throw a party!

It is often said that in Brazil, volleyball is the most popular sport. Football, they say, doesn't count as sport, as it's considered a religion!

The unique sport known as capoeira is one of the most popular pastimes amongst young Brazilians.

WHAT IS CAPOEIRA?

Capoeira is a type of martial art created by African slaves in Brazil about 400 years ago – however, it is so much more than a martial art. Capoeira is a powerful, graceful performance. It is somewhere between a choreographed acrobatic dance and a non-contact fight between two players. Music also plays an integral part in the game of capoeira. Originally designed as a symbolic representation of slaves rising up against their oppressors, capoeira has continued to be practised by Brazilians and has since become popular worldwide. People who play capoeira need to be very fit and strong, while also having all the grace of a dancer.

"When I lived on the streets, I missed my mother, our home – the other way of life. I feel that I can always rely on my mum. I loved my dad, too, but he was different. His name was Roque – he was a taxi driver, a mechanic. He died. He was an alcoholic – his life was like mine – drugs, women, partying – he didn't give a toss about anything.

When I was very young we lived here in Pelourinho, in Maciel, until the government moved us out. Our house looked out onto what is now Pedro Arcanjo Square – they have big music and dance shows for tourists there now.

I remember, a whole load of police came round to give notice. Going from house to house, aggressively, saying that on such and such a day, we would get our money. They were taking people's names down on paper, and telling us the date we had to be out.

That was the first round of evicting the people of Pelourinho for tourist developments. When we were evicted, we moved down to Gravatá (nearby). When the compensation money came through, my dad took it and left. He left us with nothing. I was about six years old then.

ALUMINIO SAYS ...

"At the end of the 1980s, the authorities appeared with this story about housing restoration.

It began at the bottom of Taboão, the lower area of Pelourinho. It soon became apparent that they

One of the big, old ruined houses in Pelourinho. Pelourinho was the location of slave auctions prior to the early 19th century, when slavery was still legal in Brazil.

were giving residents R$1,000, or even only eight hundred, and taking their houses away from them, saying they would reform them and once they were reformed, they would give them back to residents. About 1 per cent of people were given other houses, on the periphery of the city. Another 1 per cent bought themselves a piece of land. The rest of them, the majority, ended up under bridges and viaducts, on the city streets, in cardboard boxes. Most people didn't know what to do.

Hamilton's family was moved out in this first round of evictions for restoration."

Over 200 different ethnic groups co-exist in Brazil – resulting in a rich cultural heritage.

PEOPLE AND CULTURE

Brazil is a country that is proud of its multi-ethnic nature. This cultural diversity is visible via a variety of art styles, music, dance, crafts, cuisine and other traditions. However, as well as the characteristics that define Brazil's individual cultures, there are many things that unite the many peoples of Brazil. For example, 170 of the country's 184 million people speak Portuguese, the national language.

Brazilian cuisine is heavily influenced by its cultural mix. The country's national dish consists of rice, black beans and either meat or fish. This meal is called 'Feijoada'.

BAHIA AND SALVADOR

The people of the state of Bahia revel in their rich cultural mix – with a significant part of the population of African descent. Salvador is the capital of Bahia and is the third largest city in Brazil after Sao Paulo and Rio. The people of Salvador are very friendly, creative and love to have fun.

The Pelourinho, in Salvador, has the largest collection of Baroque architecture in Latin America and is a UNESCO World Heritage site. The colourful buildings and cobble-stoned streets perfectly complement the many other vibrant elements of this cultural mecca.

Brazil's population is increasing at a rapid annual rate. This has a direct impact on quality of life for people living in urban slums.

CHAPTER TWO: The Hardships of Home

Growing up in poverty can mean home – whether in a house or on the streets – can be a troublesome environment for many children and adolescents. For children who have unhappy home lives, the streets can initially seem like a way of running away from their problems and the chance to earn some money. Reality soon sets in, though, in the form of cold nights, endless hunger and long hours of work for minimal pay.

Hamilton left home because he saw the streets as a way to freedom, to escape reality.

HAMILTON SAYS ...

"When I was a little kid, I used to go to a place called Criançarte (Kid Art) at the Terreiro de Jesus with a bunch of other kids. We'd do activities – that was before I went on to the streets.

It was after my father left and we had moved to Gravatá that I began to run away from home to the streets. I was about six. The Youth Justice would pick me up, and my mum would come after me. I'm from a low-class family. Mum was a good mother but there was nothing she could do to stop me running away. I left home so I could hang out with streetkids, smoke cigarettes and cannabis and sniff glue. After being on the streets for a period, some other kids told me that Criançarte had changed to the Ibveji Project, in Rua Chile. So I went along there. At the project, we'd get

Belonging to groups like the Ibveji Project give children like Hamilton (second from left) a sense of belonging when they have severed ties with family.

paid R$5 a week if we attended school. So I went back to school – to the Mestre Pastinha School.

I loved it at Project Ibveji – there I would eat, drink and sleep. I was a street kid, I wasn't interested in anything else, just the basics. After a little while, I left everything again, and went back to the streets.

What I liked most there was theatre – a play that we did, about a street kid selling on the streets. The play was simple and practical, it caught my attention, I really liked it. I'd like to do more with the theatre sometime. I liked the coconut workshop, too – we made coconut buttons, rings, hairclips, bags, bikinis etc."

FACTS – POVERTY IN BRAZIL

Brazil has one of the highest rates of poverty in the world, including an alarmingly high rate of child poverty. The statistics speak for themselves:

• In 2004, it was estimated that 44 million Brazilians were living below the international poverty line.

• The minimum wage in Brazil is one US dollar a day. Fifty-eight million Brazilians survive on this. Many others survive on less than this.

• One in three of the people of Rio live in slums called favelas. The largest favela is home to more than 150,000 people. It lies in the heart of the wealthy neighbourhood of Gávea.

• Three children under the age of five die in Brazil every five minutes. Over 100,000 children die before their first birthday.

• The poorest 10 per cent of Brazil's population owns only 0.7 per cent of Brazil's wealth. The richest 10 per cent control 48 per cent.

Millions of Brazilians live in crowded, slum-like conditions in the poorer parts of Brazil.

"Later, I lived at Project Ibveji for a while. After that, I started to go home. The people at Project Ibveji helped me a lot. If it hadn't been for Ibveji, I wouldn't be the person I am now. They offered me a way to get away from the streets.

When I left Ibveji, I was about 13 or 14. I was back at home by then. That was when I broadened my horizons a bit. I liked to dress well then. I would go to school dressed in really smart casual gear, shoes, the lot. Ibveji had set me up with it. I really used to go to school then.

A bit later, I went back to the house my mother had rented in Gravatá. However, when I got there, I found she wasn't living there anymore. My God, I got a fright! Eventually I found out that she'd moved up the road to another place. I found her, and she took me in there. Unfortunately, my mother hadn't been able to manage to keep paying rent, and we didn't have any food so she had to leave that place, and then we were all on the streets for several days.

Next, my mother went and made a one-room shack inside the shell of a big, old, ruined house. Only the front façade of the house was standing, which is common in the historical centre. I was living on the streets at the time – I didn't live with her there.

Then I decided to go back to Ibveji, and I began to study again. That was when I got to know the gang – Juquinha, Jau and Itamar. We would sell chocolates and sweets in the streets and on the buses. I used to go to their houses, too, in their neighbourhoods, and sleep there sometimes. Itamar lived in Barros Reis, and Jau lived in Sete de Abril at the time."

Despite his years on the streets, when his mother didn't know where he was some of the time, Hamilton and his mother are very close today.

DRIVEN OUT OF HOME

In the poorer parts of Brazil the average number of people living in each household is eight. This is one of the main reasons why children leave their families and make the streets their home. Sometimes, parents simply can't cope with the number of mouths to feed. Other times, children aren't getting the attention or love they need, so they leave looking for something better.

Some children from these large families work on the streets to make money to take home. Poverty also creates other tensions that lead to children leaving home. Conflict between children and parents can lead to young people running away. Some children are also victims of domestic violence and/or sexual abuse.

Large families living in poverty sometimes willingly send their children out to work in a desperate attempt to increase the family income.

Brazilians who live on the streets and in slums are often forced to drink dirty water which causes many preventable diseases to spread.

DISEASE AND ILLNESS

Over 70 per cent of Brazil's poor have no access to clean running water, refrigeration or sewage disposal. This is a big problem in the slums (or favelas), creating the right environment for diseases to spread. Most diseases common in poverty-stricken areas, such as malaria, could have easily been prevented with improved hygiene.

It is estimated that over 40 million Brazilians do not eat well. The poor of Brazil, particularly street children, do not have the facilities to cook their own food and they cannot always afford to buy their meals. The average height of a Brazilian woman is the same as that of a 12-year-old girl in Europe or North America.

"A favela is a poor community of houses made of planks. There's more despair there, it's heavier. There's more robbery and thieving. Engomadeira – a favela I know – that's one life. Nobody can say much. Nobody can play loud music, disobey, bother neighbours. If you do, there are problems – dodgy people, craftiness. You either leave or die. If you're lucky, they'll let you leave running. The Rocinha is a ghetto, but it's different. It's very green and much calmer.

The wealthier suburbs are full of police and people in ties and suits. Chic buildings. The rich kids live there – people who have the money to do what they like.

JULIA SAYS ...

"Family breakdown is a major factor that pushes children from poorer backgrounds towards the streets in Bahia, as we can see from Hamilton's story. The lack of paternal responsibility, and often new stepfathers on the scene, creates a difficult social and economic situation. These circumstances are not uncommon in other parts of the world, be it Britain or Brazil. It is time we looked closer at some of the similarities we have in our different cultures, to see where we are all going wrong, and how we can start putting an end to the unnecessary difficulties we create for children and young people – be it at home or around our cities."

Today, Hamilton has a good relationship with his sister Bete. This photo is taken in the Rocinha where they both live.

THE FAVELAS

The families of many of Brazil's street children live in parts of cities known as favelas. Favela refers to the shanty towns that have grown up around the edge of cities. They started to appear as families began to move from the countryside in order to find work in the cities. It was only in the 1990s that efforts were made to improve the favelas with street lighting and rubbish collection. However, they still do not have the same facilities as other parts of the city.

Brazil is a country of extremes. Whilst there is great wealth and beauty in the cities and countryside, there is also a great deal of poverty. The favelas, or shanty towns, where many of the urban poor live still lack many of the most basic amenities that are available in other parts of the same city. This makes it much more likely that poor people will suffer from diseases.

Favela houses are built from cheap materials and built precariously on steep slopes.

DEATH ON THE STREETS

The figures for children dying in Brazil are much higher than for many other countries. Part of the reason for this is that there is a huge percentage of children in Brazil. It is also because poor children in Brazil are more likely to be under-nourished and vulnerable to disease. This is particularly true of children on the street. Street children also have to run the risk of being killed either by other children or by adults.

Many of the adults in Brazil who might be expected to look after these children, like police officers or security guards, are actually trying to clear them off the streets. They often use violence and even murder to clear away these children for the sake of the rest of the town.

More than 100 Brazilians are shot and killed on the city streets every day.

CHAPTER THREE: Multiple Threats

Children on the streets need to constantly keep their wits about them as a huge number of things threaten their daily existence. From disease, murder and violence to drugs, prostitution and corrupt authorities – the younger they are, the greater the risk that these youths will be caught up in something dangerous to their health, well-being and even their lives. Children and teenagers are easy prey for drug gangs looking for runners, while prostitution can seem like an easy way of making money.

HAMILTON SAYS ...

"Drugs are easy to get hold of in Salvador, and yet quite expensive. Going to sleep and waking up with the same things – it's a story that leaves me sad. Hunger is what makes me cry. When I've got no money for food and there's nothing at home. That's what really gets to me. We are day-by-day people, we're adventurers. I last cried at New Year. Giving thanks for another year of life and health, hoping for a new life. My most precious possession is my health.

The saddest day of my life occurred when the Military Police strike was on. Me and Jau were breaking into a shop, and he got shot in the stomach. I thought I was losing my

Hamilton is shown here with Marcos Paulo, a young boy (not unlike himself when he was small) from his neighbourhood.

Some of the children in the Rocinha, the district where Hamilton now lives with his mother.

friend. Thank God he didn't die though.

It's worse for girls on the street than boys. There's more risk for girls of being raped or sexually abused. Everyone looks out for themselves on the streets. You're part of a group up until a certain point. When it comes to food – each one for himself! We sleep together. The police often wake us up.

When I lived on the streets, I would go to the toilet in the bushes, in old abandoned houses, behind cars, or in bars. We rarely had baths. We used to hang about really dirty! We only got clean when we went for a swim at the beach. I didn't wash much and we often wore the same clothes. I try to stay fit and healthy now."

FACTS – PREGNANCY AND HIV

For people living in the slums and on the streets of Brazil, an obvious concern is the spread of disease, unwanted pregnancies and the threats to new mothers and their babies:

• It is estimated that about 2 million children between the ages of 10 and 15 are involved in prostitution.

• Of all the new babies born in Brazil, about 1 per cent are to mothers between the ages of 10 and 14.

• 18 per cent of all 15 to 19 year old girls are pregnant or are already mothers.

• 21 per cent of boys living on the street have had sex with another man or boy.

• Brazil has the highest number of people with HIV/AIDS in Latin America. Over half a million people in Brazil have HIV.

• For every 1,000 births, about 30 babies will die soon after being born.

Girls on the streets working as prostitutes are particularly at risk of unwanted pregnancies and contracting sexually transmitted diseases.

"I've had a few girlfriends. I've got a tattoo on my arm – the name of an Israeli girlfriend.

I don't know if I know anyone who is HIV positive or who has AIDS, that is, people don't know or don't say.

There are lots of drug gangs on our streets – I think they are a real problem. I do know some people who work for them. I used to be really scared of them. I'd leave and go elsewhere whenever I saw them. They used to tell us they killed street-kids. I know people in the favela and in Pelourinho who have died working for drug gangs. People get killed by these gangs because they get drugs and then don't pay for them, and the guys get angry and kill them.

When I lived on the streets, I was always getting beaten up by heavy groups. I'd get beaten up all over. I used to beat other kids up, too. Sometimes for money that they owed me, or for taking the mickey out of me.

I wasn't really part of a street gang when I lived on the streets. There was just a bunch of us that hung out together a lot. We'd try and stick together. Other kids on the street liked our group because we used to play jokes, have fun and get up to mischief.

I used to try and avoid fights – I would just leave if I could. We used to each carry a bit of broken glass around to defend ourselves. And we were always pinching small knives."

Hamilton has a strong sense of loyalty to his family and friends. However, he would always choose to walk away rather than fight.

DRUG GANGS

Many of the favelas are contolled by drug gangs. One of the reasons for this is that the gangs are very territorial and will always try to protect their patch. Often, the police will not attempt to enforce law and order in these areas so the drug gangs take on that role. In return, they expect loyalty from their members and for young people to do any jobs they are asked to do when required. This can range from keeping lookout, to carrying messages or becoming armed gang members ready to defend their area. Two to three police officers are killed by drug-gang members every week.

Young people cannot be arrested in Brazil unless they are actually caught committing a crime. This makes them ideal candidates for carrying drugs from one person to another. An armed gang member can earn about US$500 a month – a lot more than many legal jobs.

Many children in Brazil are employed as armed drug runners or look-outs by drug gangs.

SELLING SEX

With limited options available to them for making money, street children often resort to selling sex for money. It is usually girls who turn to prostitution, however, many boys become prostitutes as well. According to one study, Brazil has the highest rate of child prostitution in Latin America and the second highest rate in the world.

It is estimated that there are 500,000 children involved in prostitution in Brazil, although it is impossible to know the precise figure. This is because many of these young people feel ashamed of what they are doing and do not want to talk about it. Some street children have resorted to having sex with police officers in return for protection, or because they are forced to.

This eight-year-old girl is one of many children who turn to prostitution as a means of earning money on the streets of Brazil.

"I used to get harassed by the police a lot – they'd catch us sniffing glue and beat us up. Then they would take us to CAM (youth detention centre) or the Youth Justice.

I once spent two months in CAM. The police caught me with cannabis. It was before I went to the Ibveji Project – I was about 11 or 12 at the time.

I used to carry drugs for dealers from one place to another, and that was how I got caught – the drugs weren't mine.

I think drugs are a big problem in Brazil. In fact, in my opinion, drugs are the worst problem of everything that is wrong in the community. It disorganises everything and that's what leads us into poverty.

I'm not so much afraid of the police as afraid of their cowardly ways – the way they pick up on people's weak points and play dirty. I try to avoid the police. I just keep cool and quiet. Street children get raped by the police quite frequently – it happens a lot with girls. It happens with boys, too, but less often. I know of people who have been killed by the police, too – here in Pelourinho.

There are the occasional good police officers who care about street kids. Out of every ten nasty ones, there's one nicer one – a brother."

Hamilton knows that life is cheap on the streets. He believes the best way to stay out of trouble is to walk away at the first sign of it.

CAN THE POLICE BE TRUSTED?

In 1997, a special commission was set up by the Brazilian congress to look into the problem of groups of police officers acting outside the law by killing those that they saw as a threat, in particular – street children. The commission found that these groups – known as "death squads" – were active in many of Brazil's cities, especially in the favelas. Street children are most vulnerable to these 'death squads' because they have nowhere to escape to and nobody to protect them. However, anybody can be a victim of these squads.

Although these police officers are acting illegally and have killed many innocent people, (including an estimated two to five children each day), they get a lot of support from members of the public. Many believe that street children are a menace to society and that they need to be cleared off the streets. In fact, sometimes the killings are paid for by local business owners and politicians.

Many Brazilian police force are known to be corrupt. Most treat street children badly, with little regard for their welfare.

A MATTER OF SECURITY

One of the main dangers facing street children are lethal attacks from security guards. A number of shopkeepers believe that street children steal from them or put off customers, and so they pay for security guards not only to watch over the shops but also to drive away any street children who are near their shops.

Security guards are also employed by wealthier Brazilians who lived behind 'gated' communities. These guards patrol the streets and chase away any children they see. It is believed that these security guards also go into the favelas at night and attack sleeping children. Many members of the public are illegally in possession of guns to protect them from crime. A recent study indicated that the death rate by guns in Rio de Janeiro is more than 20 times higher than the United States.

This woman owns a handgun to protect her from threats to her personal safety.

CHAPTER FOUR: Fight for Survival

Hamilton would be the first to admit that you need to be tough to survive in a world where drug gangs and aggressive police dominate. Becoming part of a gang can be one way for young people on the streets to feel more secure – ensuring there is always someone looking out for them. Drugs might initially seem to offer a distraction from the perpetual cold and hunger – but the downsides are serious long-term health problems and addiction, which can drive many desperate drug-users to crime.

HAMILTON SAYS ...

"When I lived on the streets, my friends and I would share what we had with each other when any of us were hard up. Sometimes we would club together and put in one real each to buy a plate of food. Most of the time I would share with my friends, but not always

I have seen someone die before. We were at the Farol da Barra (lighthouse by the beach), having a smoke behind the rocks. Two guys were down on the beach shouting at each other. The first guy got this big rock and hurled it at the other guy's head. He went down there and then.

When street children do die, they'll be buried if they have families. I remember Laércio, a kid that used to hang out at

Hamilton sometimes had to resort to petty crime when he lived on the streets. He saw it as a necessary part of his life there.

Hamilton calls in to the home of Cultura em Movimento – an organisation working at the heart of the Rocinha's social and cultural movement.

Piedade Square. He was asleep. They killed him with a stone on his head. He was buried. His family went to his funeral.

I often dream about studying again. I would really like to be a mechanic – that was my father's profession. A normal job like that would really suit me, I think. Big businessmen inspire me.

If I was the president of Brazil, I would put an end to poverty. I would also put an end to hunger and get people off the streets. I'd also provide more medical assistance and more schooling."

FACTS – DRUGS IN BRAZIL

Street children are easily drawn to drugs. Many street children act as drug smugglers, or even take drugs themselves to help them cope with their difficult lives:

• One of the substances that street children sniff is called 'bim'. This is made from benzene – a drug which, when used long-term, can cause cancer, anaemia and harmful effects on the bone marrow and immune system.

• Pasta de coca is a paste which contains cocaine. Street children usually smoke it.

• In 1991, a survey of street children in Sao Paolo showed that 45 per cent of them used drugs every day.

• Some drugs, like Rohypnol, are popular and legal. They can be bought in most pharmacies.

• In 1992, a survey of street children showed that 100 per cent had tried drugs at one time.

• The most commonly used drugs amongst street children are glue and marijuana.

• Glue and other similar substances are inhaled from plastic or glass bottles. These inhalants are highly addictive and very damaging to the brain.

Most of Rio's slums are controlled by drug gangs. Brazilian police patrol the Rocinha district after a confrontation between rival drug gangs in 2004.

"As for what I do to earn money, I sell craft necklaces to tourists. I got started selling necklaces when I first bought a dozen of them from the people who sell them on.

The necklaces were cheap to buy and I could make up to R$50 a day in the summer season. In the winter, it was really hard to make even R$5, sometimes R$5. There are lots of other kids doing the same kind of work so it is very competitive.

Before selling jewellery, I worked in a fruit market. I didn't earn very much at all doing that, though.

I haven't committed any serious crimes before. I have robbed people and broken into a chemist. But I only did it because I was skint. I think crime is just a way of surviving. But it's also about people who've got a nerve. I do feel really sorry for the victims of crime though.

I know some people who earn a living as prostitutes. It's not cool for them. It hurts deeply, feeling that that is your life. They have to become hardened, to learn how not to feel too much.

My mother used to earn money at night, chatting up customers, as a woman of the night – a prostitute. Now she has registered for elderly assistance and receives a basic food basket each month. I love my mother more than anyone in the world. She hasn't got a mark on her, despite all her time in bars and brothels. She has had no formal education at all. She is just pure, from the heart.

When Mum got paid some compensation money from the government, she bought a little house in the favela at Engomadeira and I went to live with her. While I was living there, I worked in a fruit market, for about two years. Working, no school. There was this Dona Vilma – she was like an aunty. She liked us. We would say we had walked all the way to school, and she would believe us. We were fond of her, too. She sometimes gave us R$1. One day she asked me where I lived. I said Engomadeira. She said that her husband was opening a fruit shop there, if I wanted to work there. It was some time after, but it ended up working out."

Hamilton is not proud of some of the things he has had to do to get by on the streets. But he believes it was a necessary part of trying to stay alive.

CHILD LABOUR

Street children are often forced to work to earn money either for themselves or for their families. Jobs include washing car windscreens, shining shoes, selling souvenirs to tourists and selling food. Because most of these jobs entail working long hours through the day, these children are unable to go to school. This lessens their chances of getting a better job when they are older.

Wealthier Brazilians often employ street children to do odd jobs around their homes, such as: gardening, exercising pet dogs or cleaning swimming pools. Some older children end up moving into the houses of the people they are working for and becoming servants. Girls might be hired to become full-time maids or nannies.

Children on the streets struggle to make a living – like this young boy who is selling ice-creams.

Children as young as this group playing a Rocinha favela can be vulnerable to the many threats on the streets of Brazil.

VULNERABLE TO VIOLENCE

When a child first begins living on the street, he or she is most vulnerable to dangers, as they have not yet learned the ways of the streets. One of these dangers is, perhaps surprisingly, violence and abuse from gangs of other street children.

A child who is new to the streets might accidentally wander into an area of a city that is 'owned' by a drug gang that uses street children to do their 'dirty work'. The child on their own might also have something valuable that others want for themselves. Some older street children sometimes inflict violence on younger children to enforce their authority over them.

"We had a friend who was a bus driver – Viola. Because we used to beg on the buses, we got to know him. He'd let us on. He would pay us to clean the bus out – sweep it out and then rub this oil on the seats and stuff.

He would take us for lunch. I still see him around sometimes. He would do the Barra, Praça da Sé run. When we all got on that bus at Ibveji, it was right chaos – when we all got on together, we caused absolute mayhem! We'd get bus passes from Ibveji, and then get away without using them. We'd save them up all week, so that we could get a hot dog and some pop with them, or even to club together to smoke some cannabis. Anything for a bit of a party!

On the streets it often got very cold at night. When the buses stopped, we'd stand behind them, next to the motor, where it was really hot, to get warmed up. We would sleep huddled up together for warmth, too. When I lived on the streets, there were lots of times without help, but never without hope. I have always tried to make the best of things, to do the best I can under the circumstances. I'd go off, to be alone – maybe down to the beach to have a bit of a think, forget, smoke, look at the sea.

When I was on the street, the police would wake us up. People usually gave us some breakfast (bread and milky coffee). Sometimes we woke up and it was already sitting there beside us. Then we'd go off begging – on the buses. We'd ask for

Hamilton has been fortunate to encounter genuine people who wanted to help him. Hamilton will always be grateful to these people for their kindnesses.

leftovers in restaurants. In the afternoon, we might go and hang out at the beach. In Vitoria, there was this really nice lady – she used to give us fruit, juice, *beans and rice and chicken. Then we'd go off after money for our supper and breakfast, and then look for somewhere to sleep."*

SAFETY IN NUMBERS

Living on the streets can be lonely and it is good to have friends about. At night street children huddle up to each other for warmth and one child can keep a lookout for danger. They can also work together during the day and then share whatever they have earned.

Finding the right place to sleep is very important. Street children have to make sure that they are not in an area controlled by another gang. They also need to protect themselves from security guards and police. Children on the streets often band together for protection. Often, they will sleep in a big group with one child keeping watch.

Safety in numbers is one of the fundamental laws of the street. Children usually take turns at watching out for danger.

MURDERED IN THEIR SLEEP

On July 23, 1993, eight street children, aged between 10 and 17, were killed when three masked gunmen opened fire on a group of 50 children who were sleeping beside the Candelaria Church in the centre of Rio de Janeiro. The gunmen turned out to be policemen. One of the survivors of that attack was shot several times before the trial. Only one of the police officers was found guilty of killing the children. There was an international outcry but the killings have not stopped.

At night, street children need to find somewhere safe to sleep. The best places are normally open and public spaces. These are much easier places for one child to guard and watch while the others sleep.

A group carry the casket of one of the victims of the Candelaria Massacre in 1993.

"I used to knock about with Jau, Ricardo and Itamar – we went everywhere together. We'd go off and beg together in the streets. We'd get on the bus together – one would do one side of passengers, one the other side, asking for money – but if we saw someone getting some money out for us, first there got it! We'd swap sides if we saw an opportunity – whoever got there first got the money! It would end up in chaos!

Moabe – he's addicted to drugs now. If I had the money, I'd adopt him, take him in and bring him up. He's a great kid. He's suffered a lot, and even worse now. What I want for myself, I want for the others, too, even more for those that were part of my childhood.

I was a little kid when I started living on the streets. I'd go out all over the place. I went all over Salvador, I really had a good time doing that when I was small. The kick of getting on buses and going to various places. Sometimes I'd fall asleep on the bus, and I'd end up at the final stop. I'd just jump from bus to bus begging for money – and then, when I got to the end stop, I'd spend it on a snack and some juice. It was all a big adventure.

I imagine how my life will be in the future a lot. One day I would like to live in the country, surrounded by green and nature. I want to meet someone special and have children one day. If I could go anywhere in the world, I think I would go to Disneyland."

Hamilton dreams of turning over a new leaf and going back to continue his education.

Children from poverty-stricken families can be found wandering hungry around the slums of Brazil's cities, almost as soon as they can walk.

"He sleeps in the corner of the square,
Covered in cardboard,
Each day that passes,
He goes out in the street to earn his bread.
He doesn't know anything about
The crisis of this country.
Each day that passes,
Children, oh unhappy children.
Extermination No No No."

from a song called **EXTERMÍNIO NÃO**
(Extermination - No) – written in response to the
many death-squad killings of street children.

FACTS – WORK FOR STREET CHILDREN

In Brazil it is illegal for children under the age of 14 to work, except as an apprentice. However, many street children younger than 14 have to work in order to survive:

• The International Labour Office (part of the UN) has estimated that about 16 per cent of 10 to 14 year olds are working in Brazil.

• 17 per cent of all workers in Brazil are children or teenagers. While in northeastern Brazil, the figure is nearer to 30 per cent.

• 65 per cent of working children work more than the maximum number of hours per day.

• 80 per cent of child workers earn less than the minimum wage ($USD1 per day).

• Only 25 per cent of child workers get help with education and social security.

• It is also estimated that nearly 8,000 Brazilian children are working in unhealthy or painful conditions at any given time.

Many children on the streets of Brazil work up to 14 hours a day just to earn enough for a day's food.

CHAPTER FIVE: A Better Life?

Despite all he has endured in his life so far, Hamilton has remained upbeat and enthusiastic about his future prospects. There is no doubt that he wants a better life than the one he is currently living. He is well aware that there is no future for a young person on the streets – and that things like drugs, prostitution, violence and crime only succeed in damaging young lives and suppressing their true potential.

Hamilton now spends a lot of time in the Terreiro district where a lot of tourist-based work can be found.

HAMILTON SAYS ...

I worry about the future – I don't want things to go wrong, I don't want to mess up my life. At the moment I am looking forward to changing my lifestyle, to carnival ... and hopefully meeting a girl, the one for me.
If I could have one wish, it would be that I could get out of this life that I'm in now and move on to better things.

JULIA SAYS ...

"It is time for us all to question why the world is so unbalanced and what causes the extremes of poverty and wealth that we are becoming so accustomed to hearing about and seeing on TV. We can become informed, about youth, about Brazil, about our world, and become active in doing what we can, at home or elsewhere, to change attitudes for the better."

Like millions of other young Brazilians, Hamilton has had a difficult life so far. However, he now claims to be happier than he has ever been – living with his mother in the Rocinho district. Hamilton's goals include developing his jewellery business and going back to study as soon as he is able to.

YOUTH DETENTION CENTRES

Street children who have been arrested for petty crimes are not put into jail with adult criminals, but are placed in Youth Detention Centres. The theory is that, in these institutions, youths will receive the appropriate care and be given the chance to get some education.

There have been accusations of children being beaten by guards who work in the centres. Children can also be locked in their cells for several days without any exercise or the chance to meet others. The cells are often kept in a filthy condition and sickness is common among inmates. Children who commit more serious crimes are placed in jails reserved specifically for young people.

This inmate at Salvador's jail for minors was jailed for attempting to murder a boy for stealing his sneakers.

HELPING STREET CHILDREN TO LEARN

For many street children, education and job training is the only way that they will escape from the streets and make new lives for themselves. Many non-governmental organisations (NGOs) that work with the street children of Brazil are concerned with ensuring that these young people have good educational opportunities. For example, ChildHope UK is working in the favelas of Rio creating opportunities for young people so that they can train for a job.

These children once lived on the streets but have since enrolled in one of the many skills-training courses implemented by charities and NGOs.

PROTECTING THE STREET CHILDREN

Children on the streets of Brazil's cities are amongst the most vulnerable members of society. Not only do they have to look after themselves every day but they also have to face daily threats from death squads and corrupt police who are paid by businesses and local politicians to clear them off the streets. For many years, the Brazilian government did little to help street children. Many members of the Brazilian ruling élite saw the children as little more than vermin or criminals.

It was only in the 1990s that the Brazilian government began to take action to help protect street children. In 1990, Congress passed the Statute of the Child and Adolescent. It was supposed to allow street children the "right to freedom, respect, dignity as a human being" as well as the "right to be in a public and community space". The statute also says that children can only be arrested if they are seen committing a crime. This was supposed to protect them from corrupt police. However, it also means that drug gangs have exploited this change in the law by using children to smuggle drugs.

Various government schemes have attempted to tackle the problem of sub-standard education in many parts of Brazil. However, the problems still persist.

LEARNING OPPORTUNITIES

One of the main reasons why children do not go to school is simply because their families cannot afford to send them. Although education is free, the children can't earn money for their families while they are at school.

In 1991, the Brazilian government began to encourage street children to return to school. President Cardosa promised to open 5,000 new schools for the children of poor families. By the time the president was removed after accusations of fraud, it was discovered that only 20 of these schools had been built and even less were open. In the end only 5,000 children benefitted from this project.

While there are some police who genuinely care about protecting the rights of street children, many more are employed by business-owners to clear children off the streets by whatever means necessary.

In 1998, the president launched a scheme to get children living in poverty back to school. This was done by offering the parents of poor children R$25 (about £12) per month for each child they sent back to school. The idea behind this scheme was that this money would replace the money that the child would have earned on the streets. There have been reports that some parents are not getting the money that is owed to them, or that they are keeping the money but still sending their children out to work in the evenings.

ERADICATING CHILD LABOUR

Getting children back to school will help to make sure that they do not have to work in order to survive. The Brazilian government has made it an aim to get rid of child labour completely. In 1988 the government made it illegal for children under the age of 18 to work at night or to do dangerous jobs. They also made it illegal for children under the age of 16 to have any kind of job.

The 'Program to Eradicate Child Labour' (PETI) was created by the Brazilian government in 1998,. It was given the aim of eliminating child labour completely. By the end of 2000, PETI had helped over 300,000 children to escape work obligations or enforced work.

THE CHILD AND ADOLESCENT ACT

Until the passing of the Child and Adolescent Act, no child in Brazil, whether they were street children or not, had any rights that were written down in a law. The Statute of the Child and Adolescent made it clear for the first time not only that children needed special protection and consideration but also that they had the right to expect this special treatment. The Act also

made it an obligation of the Brazilian government to take particular care of children who are vulnerable – including street children.

The Act called for the creation of two types of councils to ensure that the needs of young people are looked after. The first type is Guardianship Councils which were supposed to be set up all over Brazil to listen to the needs of individual children and make recommendations for how they could improve their lives. The other councils to be introduced were local Children's Rights Councils. These councils were meant to decide on policies that affected children and distribute money to those who work with them. These two councils have been set up in many parts of Brazil. However, there are some parts of the country where they have not been set up or they do not have as much power as they are supposed to have. Much of this is due to the fact that some parts of Brazil are poorer than others and have a larger number of children that need more help from the councils.

Shockingly, children on Brazil's streets can end up in employment as young as three or four years old. The girl below is making her living by washing car windscreens.

CHAPTER SIX: Those Who Help

Many aid organisations and charities that deal with children have been working alongside the Brazilian government trying to help the street children. Some of them are Brazilian in origin. There are also some international organisations that work with street children all over the world, including Brazil. Some of these bodies are known as non-governmental organisations (NGOs) and include the Red Cross, Save the Children and Oxfam. They rely on private donations from richer nations to do their work.

Poverty can drive hungry children to forage for food at the local dump. In hot climates such as Brazil's, rotten and decomposing food can be a breeding ground for bacteria and disease.

It works with children in Africa, Latin America and Eastern Europe. In Brazil, ChildHope works most closely with those children who are victims of violence or are involved in prostitution. Their work includes a young person's theatre project in Brazil's favelas.

Founded in 1997, Estrela is based in Britain and works in the city of Salvador in Brazil. The group works with youth and communities in Brazil and Britain to promote

CHILDHOPE AND ESTRELA

ChildHope UK was established in 1990, to defend the rights of street children around the world and provide opportunities for them to create a better future for themselves.

inclusive development and intercultural understanding. One of Estrela's main projects is to support small-scale projects in Salvador that involve theatre art or dance.

CULTURA EM MOVIMENTO

Cultura em Movimento (Culture in Movement) is a prominent cultural/arts organisation based in Salvador, Brazil. The organisation grew out of an activist organisation called SOS Children of the Historical Centre. SOS fought against the government scheme of the late-1980s that evicted people from their homes with the promise that houses would be returned to their residents once they were restored. This promise was only fulfilled to a small percentage of those affected (see pages 16–17). SOS rallied the people to rise up and fight against the restoration project, to say no to

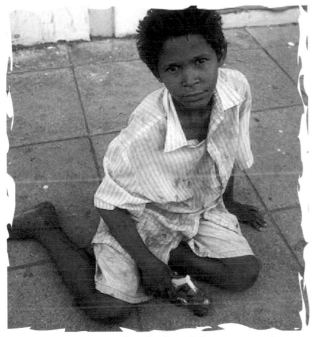

Living on the streets can be a lonely and desperate experience for children.

what was being offered. In time, the organisation relocated to the Rocinha and evolved into a cultural movement, celebrating the rich cultural legacy of the region. Cultura em Movimento is led by Aluminio (co-interviewer) and holds regular reggae music events that have become renowned internationally and which are inclusive to all people of the region, whether they live in houses or on the streets. The events are ruled by an atmosphere of peace – providing a haven from the aggressive elements of life on the streets.

THE NATIONAL MOVEMENT OF STREET CHILDREN

The National Movement of Street Children (MNMMR) was founded in 1985. This organisation was created by political activists and people who were already working with street children. The idea behind the Movement is to allow children to organise and look after themselves better whilst still living on the streets. The Movement has about 3,000 'Street Educators' who have reached tens of thousands of street children. The children are encouraged to form groups called a *núcleos*. In addition to creating these groups, the Movement also makes sure that the 1990 Statute of the Child and Adolescent is never forgotten.

CASE STUDY – MOTHER CITY

Many of these organisations work in conjunction with the Brazilian government and also with local governments to provide support for street children. One project that has been funded by the government is *Cidade Mãe* (Mother City). This project is based in the city of Salvador in Northeast Brazil. The project aims to give training to young poor people so that they might be able to find themselves a better-paid job and so escape poverty. As well as providing training for young people who are not in school, Mother City also runs after-school clubs for those who are lucky enough to attend school.

Mother City is also concerned with reducing the number of 14–18-year-olds who become addicted to drugs or become pregnant. This is done through health, sex-education and counselling programmes.

MAKING BRAZIL FAIRER

This will only happen if all Brazilian governments in the future make sure that the benefits of economic growth are more evenly spread across all parts of Brazilian society. In the past, the poorest members of Brazil did not gain as much as the more wealthy. If poorer families become a little more wealthy then there is less need for children to go out to work or for young people to be forced out on to the streets.

The current Brazilian government is the Workers' Party. In 2002 their candidate for president promised that he would give land to the landless poor. When he won, he began a series of reforms. This included giving land to many thousands of people who did not own any land.

NUMBERS OF STREET CHILDREN

As long as the Brazilian government and aid organisations try to help street children either directly or through their families, then their lives will improve and the numbers on the streets will fall. After events like the Candeleria massacre in 1993, Brazilian

Most of the street children in Brazil are boys but the number of girls seems to be constantly increasing.

people are slowly changing their minds about street children. More and more people are realising that these children need help rather than punishment for being poor. This will then put more pressure on the government to do more.

However, one thing that might mean that the number of street children actually increases will be the continually growing population of Brazil. The population is currently around 184 million. According to the United Nations this is due to increase to nearly 250 million by 2050. This will be almost entirely due to more children being born. This will put a strain on the schools, housing, jobs and transport of Brazil. If the country cannot take this strain, then it is possible that the number of street children may actually go up rather than down.

GETTING RID OF CORRUPTION

The lives of street children cannot begin to improve until the way that Brazil is governed is changed. The Brazilian government wants the country to become a more economically powerful nation, with a stronger voice in the United Nations. This can only be done through tapping into the talents of all Brazilian people, young and old, rich and poor. Members of the Brazilian government know that this cannot be achieved while there are huge numbers of poor and unskilled people in both the cities and in rural areas. Providing educational opportunities is the most important way to help the poor. However, street gangs often use guns to settle arguments between different groups. The drug trade also makes it almost impossible to help young people out of poverty. The police force often do nothing to tackle these two major problems. Guns, drugs and police corruption must be eliminated before other government programmes will really start to work.

STREET CHILDREN AROUND THE WORLD

Brazil is not the only country in the world to have a large number of children living on the streets. Countries that have been at war with neighbouring

After the scandalous Candelaria massacre, the people of Brazil finally started to recognise that their country, and in particular their young people, were In the midst of a crisis.

nations or are fighting a civil war will see an increase in the number of street children who have who have become separated from their families escaping from war. Some children find that their parents have died. In both cases children will head towards the nearest town to find work and food. Countries such as Nepal and Ethiopia have street children as a direct result of conflict.

Just like Brazil, it is poverty and inequality around the world, particularly in developing countries like Kenya and Bangladesh, that forces children onto the streets. Noticeable groups of children have begun to reappear on the streets of the cities of Europe. Countries like Russia and Romania have children living on the streets of Moscow and Bucharest.

HOW YOU CAN HELP

1. BUY FAIRTRADE GOODS
Buying Fairtrade goods helps to ensure that farmers in poor countries are paid a good price for the crops they grow. Crops that are grown in Brazil include coffee and cocoa.

2. TWIN WITH A BRAZILIAN SCHOOL
When your school is twinned with a school from another country, pupils from each school swap letters and pictures. If your school is not already twinned with another, ask your teacher to find out if there is a way to twin with a Brazilian school.

3. MAKE A DONATION
There are many charities, like ChildHope UK and Estrela, who are working to make the lives of Brazilian street children better. You can make a donation to help them with their work. Always make sure you choose a registered charity.

4. SPREAD THE WORD
Many of the charities and organisations that work with Brazilian street children can provide speakers to come to your school. Ask your teacher if he or she can help with organising a talk.

5. TALK TO OTHER GROUPS
If you belong to a group like the scouts, guides or the Woodcraft Folk, then you can make links with similar groups in Brazil. Talk to your group leader about this. If you belong to a church group, then you might be able to make contact with other churches in Brazil. Talk to your pastor or group leader.

GLOSSARY

ABANDONED Deserted or left behind permanently.

AMENITIES Useful or desirable features of a place.

APPRENTICE Person learning a trade from a skilled employer.

CAPOEIRA Type of graceful yet disciplined martial
art that originated amongst Brazilian slaves and is still commonly practiced in Brazil, and around the world, today.

CARNIVAL The most famous event of the Brazilian calendar – a party that takes place on the streets of Brazil's cities every February and lasts for five days.

CHOREOGRAPHED A composed sequence of dance steps and moves.

CONFLICT Serious disagreement, struggle or fight.

CONGRESS National law-making body.

CORRUPTION Acting dishonestly in return for money or personal gain.

DEATH SQUAD Name attributed to group of police officers acting outside the law by killing street children just for being on the streets.

DEMOCRACY Form of government where the people have a voice in the exercise of power.

ECONOMY The state of a country or region according to the production and consumption of goods and services and the supply of money.

ECO-TOURISM Tourism directed towards unspoiled natural environments and intended to support conservation efforts.

ELITE Group of people considered to be superior in a society.

ENFORCE Cause something to happen by force.

EVICTED Legally forced to remove from one's home.

EXPLOITED Derive benefit from something unfairly and at someone's expense.

FAVELA House built in the slums, made of cheap materials and supported by poles (because they are usually built on unstable ground, eg: sides of hills).

FORAGE Search widely for food or provisions.

IMMIGRANTS People who come to live permanently in a foreign country.

IMPLEMENTED Started something.

INTIMIDATION Bullying or treating someone aggressively in order to force them into a certain situation or decision.

LABOUR Work.

MASSACRE Indiscriminate and brutal slaughter of people.

MILITARY POLICE Uniformed police officers that operate in large groups.

MULATTO Mixed race.

NON-GOVERNMENTAL ORGANISATION (NGO) Non-profit organisation that works to help people in developing countries who are living in difficult situations.

PERIPHERY The edge of something.

POLICIES Courses of action proposed by an organisation or individual.

PROSTITUTION A person who exchanges sex for money.

REFORMED Something that has been changed for the better.

RESTORATION The action of renovating or restoring something that is in need of repair.

SALVATION Deliverance from sin by belief in religion, typically Christianity.

SAMBA Brazilian dance of African origin.

SCANDALOUS Something that is morally wrong.

SMUGGLE Move goods illegally into or out of a country.

TERRITORIAL Of or relating to the ownership of land or sea.

TRUANT Pupil who stays away from school without leave or excuse.

UNDERNOURISHED Not having enough food for good health.

VERMIN Wild mammals or rodents which are harmful to crops or which carry disease.

VULNERABLE Exposed to being harmed, either emotionally or physically.

FURTHER INFORMATION

CHILDHOPE UK
An international, UK-based, non-governmental organisation committed to working with children who are neglected by their families, communities and governments and are the most vulnerable to violence, exploitation and disease. www.childhopeuk.org

ESTRELA UK
A UK-based organisation that works with youth and communities in Brazil and Britain to promote inclusive development and intercultural understanding. Estrela is involved with many schemes and projects that assist street children and promote more widespread understanding of the issues facing Brazil, such as: setting up links between schools in Brazil and Britain; organising talks and workshops on Brazil and street children in Britain and assisting arts/music-based projects to develop that incorporate the talents of street children.Any donations can be contributed towards helping young people like Hamilton get off the streets. Email: estrela@atarde.com.br

NATIONAL MOVEMENT OF STREET CHILDREN (Movimento Nacional de Meninos e Meninas de Rua, or MNMMR). A voluntary NGO founded in 1985 by activists and 'street educators' who sought to empower and organise street children in their own environment. www.icrc.org

JUBILEE ACTION
Jubilee Action is an international human-rights charity, dedicated to protecting children at risk, defending persecuted Christians and combating poverty. www.jubileeaction.co.uk

TASK BRAZIL
Task Brasil Trust is a UK registered charity established in 1992. Under the supervision of its small London office, Task Brasil's projects in Brazil improve the lives and support the needs of children and pregnant teenage girls living on the streets of Brazil. www.taskbrasil.org.uk